NOT NEAR NORMAL
THE PARANORMAL

WEREWOLVES
AND OTHER SHAPE-SHIFTERS

by Ruth Owen

Consultant: Troy Taylor
President of the American Ghost Society

BEARPORT
PUBLISHING

New York, New York

Credits

Cover and Title Page, © Zacarias Pereira da Mata/Shutterstock, cynoclub/Shutterstock, and © Kim Jones; 4–5, © Peter Hansen/Shutterstock and © AF archive/Alamy; 6, © mlorenz/Shutterstock; 6–7, © AF archive/Alamy; 8–9, © Kamira/Shutterstock and © Kim Jones; 11, © Kim Jones; 12, © thawats butterfly/Shutterstock; 13, © Jaroslaw Grudzinski/Shutterstock; 14, © carroteater/Shutterstock and Sibrikov Valery/Shutterstock; 14–15, © Kim Jones; 16–17, © Gerard Lacz Images/Superstock; 18–19, © Piyathep/Shutterstock and Bob Orsillo/Shutterstock; 21, © Telemack/istockphoto; 22–23, © Giancarlo Gagliardi/Shutterstock and © Krzysztof Wikto/Shutterstock; 24, © Tippett Studio; 25, © Holly Kuchera/Shutterstock and © AF archive/Alamy; 27, © Rex Features; 28L, © greglith/Shutterstock; 28R, © outdoorsman/Shutterstock; 29TL, © Martin B. Withers/FLPA; 29TR, © AF archive/Alamy; 29BL, © Stanislav Duben/Shutterstock; 29BR, © sergey23/Shutterstock.

Publisher: Kenn Goin
Editorial Director: Adam Siegel
Creative Director: Spencer Brinker
Design: Emma Randall
Editor: Mark J. Sachner
Photo Researcher: Ruby Tuesday Books Ltd

Library of Congress Cataloging-in-Publication Data

Owen, Ruth, 1967–
  Werewolves and other shape-shifters / by Ruth Owen.
      p. cm. — (Not near normal: the paranormal)
  Includes bibliographical references and index.
  ISBN 978-1-61772-695-8 (library binding) — ISBN 1-61772-695-8 (library binding)
  1. Werewolves. 2. Shapeshifting. I. Title.
  GR830.W4O94 2013
  398.24'54—dc23
                            2012038864

For more information, write to Bearport Publishing Company, Inc., 45 West 21st Street, Suite 3B, New York, New York 10010. Printed in the United States of America.

10 9 8 7 6 5 4 3 2

Contents

The Creature at the Window

Scratch. Scratch. Scratch. Delburt Gregg woke up.

It was a hot, stormy night in Greggton, Texas. Before going to sleep, Delburt had moved her bed beside a window, hoping to catch a breeze. Now, just inches from her, something was scratching at the screen.

Suddenly, a flash of lightning lit up the window. Looking in at Delburt was a huge, hairy, wolflike face with sharp **fangs** and glowing eyes. In an instant, the creature turned and ran into some bushes.

Terrified, Delburt anxiously watched from her window. Would the beast return? Instead of a wolflike creature emerging from the bushes, however, Delburt saw a very tall man suddenly appear and run out of sight.

What did Delburt Gregg see that hot summer night in July 1958? A wolf? A man? Or something not near normal—a **werewolf**!

The Man Wolf

The word *werewolf* comes from two words in **Old English**: *wer*, which means "man," and *wulf*, which means "wolf."

Becoming a Werewolf

According to legend, people are not born as werewolves. Instead, some people are said to choose to become werewolves by rubbing a magic **ointment** made from **poisonous** plants on their bodies. In other stories, people turn into werewolves when they wear a wolf **hide** or put on a belt made from wolf skin.

Some tales tell of people who do not choose to change into killer beasts. These people become werewolves when they are bitten, but not killed, by a werewolf. After the attack, the victim may at first believe that he or she has made a lucky escape. The next time there is a **full moon**, however, the victim changes into a howling, bloodthirsty werewolf. The **vicious** beast is doomed forever to hunt and kill each time a full moon appears in the night sky.

Werewolf Water

One old story says that it's possible to become a werewolf by drinking rainwater that has gathered in the paw print of a wolf.

Transformation

What does it feel like to turn into a werewolf? No one knows for sure, but according to stories, a person—or werewolf—might describe it like this:

A Werewolf's Diary

A full moon lit up the night sky. Suddenly, I felt a grinding pain as my bones began to stretch and change into the shape of a wolf. All over my body, rough, wiry hair sprouted from my skin.

I smashed through the door of my house, running faster than I'd ever run before. My glowing red eyes saw someone walking in the distance. He turned, saw me, and let out a terrible scream—but I felt no pity.

I was so hungry, and it was time to feed!

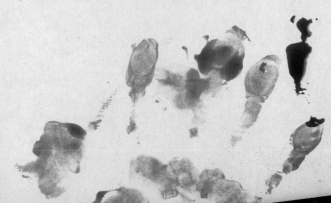

Terrifying Changes

As a person changes into a werewolf, his or her hands and feet become paws with sharp claws. The person's face stretches into a long **snout** with fangs, while ears grow pointed and wolflike.

The Signs of a Werewolf

If werewolves walk among us, what signs can help a person tell if a neighbor is secretly a killer beast? One clue to look for is a strange **injury** that seems to have happened overnight.

Old stories say that if a werewolf is wounded, the injury can still be seen when the creature changes back into its human form. For example, in some tales, people have cut off a werewolf's paw during an attack. The next day, they discover that one of their neighbors is missing a hand!

Hundreds of years ago, some people believed that werewolves turned their fur-covered skin inside out when they returned to their human forms. To check if a neighbor was a werewolf, people would cut open the **suspect**'s skin to look for fur.

A hairy palm is one sign of a werewolf.

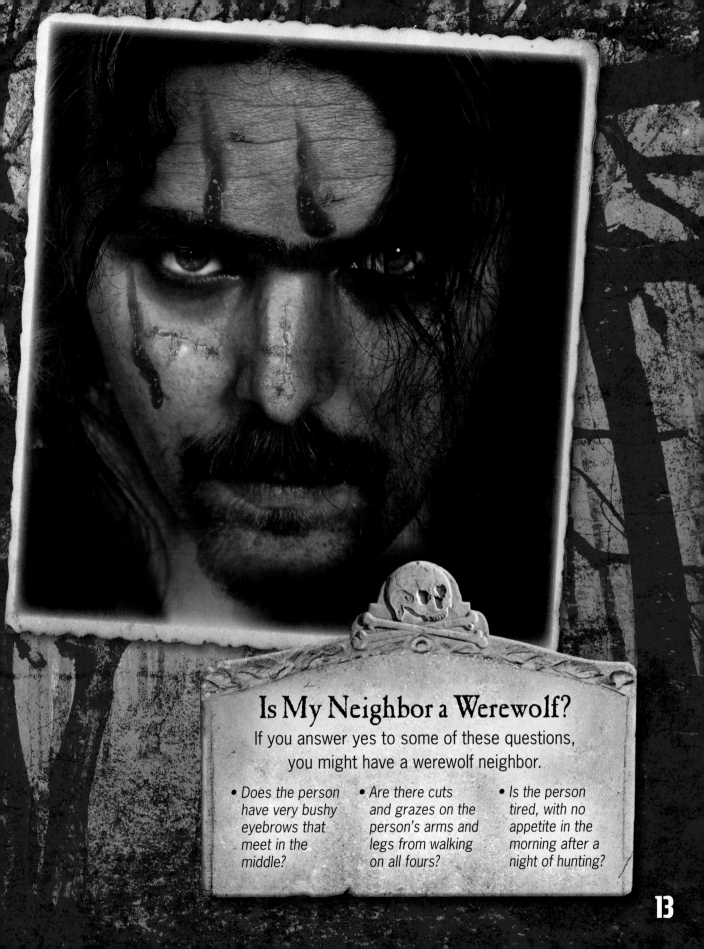

Is My Neighbor a Werewolf?

If you answer yes to some of these questions, you might have a werewolf neighbor.

- Does the person have very bushy eyebrows that meet in the middle?

- Are there cuts and grazes on the person's arms and legs from walking on all fours?

- Is the person tired, with no appetite in the morning after a night of hunting?

Can a Werewolf Be Killed?

Once people are sure they have found a werewolf, legends say there is only one certain way to end its **reign of terror**. The evil beast must be killed!

To be sure of ending a werewolf's life, the creature's head should be cut off and its heart removed from its body. Hanging the beast or tying it to a **stake** and burning it are also good ways to rid the world of the evil killer.

If the creature is in werewolf form at the moment of death, it will often change back into a person. Then all that is left of the terrifying beast is a human **corpse**.

Silver Bullets

Many werewolf legends and stories say that a silver bullet or silver knife will kill a werewolf.

The Beast of Gévaudan

Terrible stories of werewolf attacks have been told around the world for hundreds of years. In the 1760s, many people were attacked and killed by a bloodthirsty creature in the Gévaudan (*zhay*-voh-DAWN) region of France.

The killings in Gévaudan were so savage that over time stories arose that the killer was actually a werewolf. **Witnesses** who saw the vicious creature described it as a giant wolf that was the size of a cow. Hunters tried to shoot the giant beast on many occasions, but it always escaped.

Determined to stop the attacks, in June 1767, hundreds of hunters searched the countryside for the creature. One of the hunters, Jean Chastel, finally shot a huge, wolflike animal.

In the dead animal's stomach, Chastel found the **collarbone** of a young girl. Had he killed a werewolf? After the animal's body was buried, the Beast of Gévaudan was never seen again.

Gévaudan, France

Wolf or Werewolf?

The Beast of Gévaudan is thought to have killed about 60 people. Some believed the beast was simply a huge wolf. Others thought the ferocious, bloodthirsty creature had to be a werewolf.

The Terrifying Taw

People have claimed to spot werewolves all over the world. In the mountains of Myanmar (*myahn*-MAR), in Southeast Asia, people live in fear of werewolves that appear from the jungle. The flesh-eating creatures are called taws.

In one famous story from 1960, a government official named Harold Young was visiting a mountain village. Young saw a horrible dark-haired beast with fangs and small red eyes attacking a woman. Young believed it was a taw. He shot at the beast, but it ran off into the jungle, leaving a trail of blood.

The next morning, Young followed the bloody trail into the jungle. It eventually led him back to one of the village huts. Expecting to see the taw inside the hut, Young was shocked to find a dead man. When Young examined the body, he found a bullet from his own gun in the man's side!

Myanmar

Asia

N
W — E
S

Indian Ocean

A Final Transformation?

How had a bullet from Harold Young's gun killed the villager? Young believed he knew the answer. The dead man was a taw! As the horrible creature died, it had transformed back into its human form.

The Werewolf of Bedburg

One of history's most horrifying werewolf stories took place in Bedburg, Germany, during the 1500s. A farmer named Peter Stumpf killed—and then ate—several people in the town where he lived.

After 25 years of committing terrible murders, Stumpf was finally captured. During his trial, Stumpf claimed that the devil had given him a magic belt. He said that when he wore the belt, he became a ferocious werewolf.

Peter Stumpf was sentenced to death for his crimes. His arms and legs were broken, and his head was cut off. Finally, his body was burned. All that remained of the Werewolf of Bedburg was a pile of ash!

An Unbelievable Change

Was Peter Stumpf really a werewolf? One story says Stumpf was captured after a group of men with dogs tracked down a wolf that had carried off a young boy. As the men watched in disbelief, the wolf changed from a wild beast into Peter Stumpf.

Bedburg, Germany

N

W — E

S

Europe

Atlantic Ocean

Shape-shifters

Werewolves are a kind of **shape-shifter**—a creature that can turn from one form to another. In legends from around the world, humans shape-shift to take the form of wild animals. In India, people tell stories of "weretigers." In tales from Africa, people may change into lions, hyenas, leopards, and crocodiles.

In North America, the Navajo people tell stories about shape-shifters called "skinwalkers." These evil witches can take the form of wolves, coyotes, foxes, crows, or owls. When a skinwalker is in animal form, he or she has the same skills and powers as the wild animal. Legends say that if a skinwalker looks deep into a person's eyes, the skinwalker can make the person fall ill and die.

Super-fast Skinwalkers

Skinwalkers can move very fast. Witnesses say they have seen these creatures running at 60 miles per hour (97 kph)!

The *Twilight* Werewolves

Terrifying werewolves and other shape-shifters have appeared in many books and movies over the years. In the series of *Twilight* books, the character Jacob Black and other members of his Quileute Indian tribe are shape-shifters. The characters change from their human forms into giant timber wolves in less than a second.

To create the transformations for the *Twilight* movies, artists working on computers blended film of the real-life human actors with **computer-generated images** of wolves. To make sure the wolves they created moved and acted in a realistic way, the artists watched real wolves to see how they jump, run, and fight.

A *Twilight* computer artist spends time with a
tame wolf as part of his research for the movies.

Wolf Eyes

The *Twilight* film team wanted Jacob Black's wolf eyes to look like his human eyes. Taylor Lautner, the actor who played Jacob, had close-up shots of his eyeballs filmed. They were then blended with computer-generated wolf eyes.

Members of the *Twilight* wolf pack in their human form

Fact or Fiction?

Today, most people understand that wolves are shy animals that rarely attack humans. Yet legends about bloodthirsty werewolves have existed for thousands of years. How did these stories get started?

Long ago, people were afraid of wolves because they believed that the animals were vicious creatures that hid in dark forests waiting to attack people. Popular fairy tales even told of the "big bad wolf" that killed and ate people. The fear of these powerful, meat-eating creatures may have led to the spread of werewolf stories.

We will never know for sure exactly how the legends began. However, one thing is certain. No one has ever proved that werewolves exist—but no one has proved that they don't!

Real-life Wolf People

A small number of people have a rare condition called **hypertrichosis**. These people grow hair all over their faces and bodies. Perhaps stories of werewolves began when people saw a hairy person with hypertrichosis.

Larry and Danny Gomez are brothers who were both born with hypertrichosis.

Werewolves and Other Shape-shifters Around the World

If there's any chance that werewolves and other shape-shifters exist, it makes sense to know who's who in the world of bloodthirsty flesheaters. Check out these gruesome creatures to find out who eats what, and to learn where some people think they are likely to show up next.

Jé-rouge (JAY-ROOJ)

Location: Haiti

Description: Hairy half-human, half-animal beast with red eyes

Favorite food: Humans

Behavior: The Jé-rouge wakes a mother in the dead of night and asks if it can feed on her child. The mother is so sleepy, she sometimes says yes!

Böxenwolf (BUK-suhn-wulf)

Location: The Schaumberg region of Germany

Description: A böxenwolf is a person who becomes a wolf when he or she puts on a special belt that was a gift from the devil. The transformed creature looks like a regular wolf.

Favorite food: Humans

Behavior: A böxenwolf thinks like a human but has a wolf's excellent eyesight and sense of smell. It can also run very fast.

Bouda (BOO-duh)

Location: Many countries in Africa

Description: A witch with the power to change into a hyena at night

Favorite food: Dead bodies

Behavior: A bouda visits graveyards to steal and eat dead bodies.

El Lobizón (EL loh-bee-ZOHN)

Location: Argentina

Description: A large, muscular, hairy, doglike creature that walks on two legs

Favorite food: Chickens and cows

Behavior: El lobizón raids farms to catch and kill livestock.

Hamrammr (HAHM-rahm-ur)

Location: Iceland

Description: A man who can change into many different animals

Favorite food: Deer, rabbits, birds—any kind of animal that can be hunted

Behavior: A hamrammr can change into the animal that was his last meal. When in animal form, the hamrammr has the speed or skills, such as flight, of the animal he last ate!

Kitsune (kit-SOON-uh)

Location: Japan

Description: A fox with magical powers that may have up to nine tails

Favorite food: Small animals

Behavior: A kitsune can shape-shift into a human, usually a beautiful woman, but the human form still has a fox's tail.

Glossary

collarbone (KOL-ur-*bohn*) one of the two bones that joins the breastbone to the shoulder blades and makes up part of the shoulder

computer-generated images (kuhm-PYOO-tur-JEN-uh-*rayt*-id IM-uh-jiz) pictures made by computer technology

corpse (KORPS) a dead body

fangs (FANGZ) long, pointed teeth

full moon (FUL MOON) the moon as it appears when the entire surface facing Earth is illuminated

hide (HIDE) animal skin

hypertrichosis (hye-pur-tri-KOH-sis) abnormal hair growth over the body or parts of the body

injury (IN-juh-ree) harm done to a person's body

legend (LEJ-uhnd) a story handed down from long ago that is often based on some facts but cannot be proven true

ointment (OINT-muhnt) a thick, sometimes greasy substance that is put on the skin, usually to heal or protect it

Old English (OHLD ING-lish) the early form of English that was spoken until about the year 1100

poisonous (POI-zuhn-uss) able to kill or harm someone if eaten

reign of terror (RAYN UHV TER-ur) a period of time in which violence occurs

savage (SAV-ij) wild, dangerous, and fierce

shape-shifter (SHAYP-*shif*-tur) a person or creature with the ability to change from one physical form into another at will

snout (SNOUT) the long, front part of an animal's head that sticks out; it includes the nose and usually the jaws and mouth

stake (STAYK) a strong pole with a sharp point at the end

suspect (SUHSS-pekt) someone thought to have committed a crime

vicious (VISH-uhss) fierce and dangerous

werewolf (WAIR-wulf) a person who changes for periods of time into a wolf or wolflike creature, usually when there is a full moon

witnesses (WIT-niss-iz) people who tell what they saw

Bibliography

Curran, Bob. *Werewolves: A Field Guide to Shapeshifters, Lycanthropes, and Man-Beasts.* Franklin Lakes, NJ: New Page Books (2009).

Curran, Robert. *The Werewolf Handbook.* Hauppauge, NY: Barrons Educational Series (2010).

Steiger, Brad. *The Werewolf Book: The Encyclopedia of Shape-Shifting Beings.* Canton, MI: Visible Ink Press (2011).

Summers, Monatgue. *The Werewolf in Lore and Legend.* Minneapolis, MN: Dover (2003).

Read More

Ganeri, Anita. *Werewolves and Other Shape-Shifters (The Dark Side).* New York: Rosen (2011).

Pipe, Jim. *Werewolves (Tales of Horror).* New York: Bearport (2007).

Townsend, John. *Werewolf Attack (Crabtree Contact).* New York: Crabtree (2009).

Learn More Online

To learn more about werewolves, visit
www.bearportpublishing.com/NotNearNormal

Index

About the Author

Ruth Owen has been developing, editing, and writing children's books for more than ten years. She lives in Cornwall, England, just minutes from the ocean. Ruth loves gardening and caring for her family of llamas.